MARGARET ROBERTS HERB SERIES

Cooking with Winter Herbs

Illustrated by
Sanmarie Harms

David Bateman

© Margaret Roberts 1986

Originally published by Lowry Publishers.
This edition published in 1989 by David Bateman Ltd,
'Golden Heights', 32–34 View Road, Glenfield,
Auckland 10, New Zealand

Reprinted 1992

ISBN 0 86777 132 1

A David Bateman book
Printed in Hong Kong by Colorcraft

Contents

Introduction

You've heard it before, but the fact remains – we are what we eat, and nowadays more and more people are anxious to experience continuous physical health and a high level of fitness.

It is not only cranks and health fanatics who look with care to their diet; today the health-conscious youth, housewives and mothers concerned about their families' health, and even those of the older generation who can no longer accept the aches and pains their senior years are supposedly thrusting upon their shoulders, all are taking a careful look at what they eat. This book is for those people. It is a book with which to live, to work and to survive. It is not just a recipe book but a way of life – it is a health book, a food for thought book, because as we become more aware of what we eat, so we need to find and experience what is right for us, what will build our bodies to that perfect health.

In the winter months a certain type of diet is needed by the body. This includes foods which generate warmth and assist the circulation, and herbs which aid assimilation of food, keep the body free of toxins, and build up resistance to infection. These properties are contained in the following mouth-watering recipes. All have been tried and tested in my Herbal Centre Country Kitchen, but some may need small adjustments depending, for example, on the size of eggs used, the creaminess of the milk, the juiciness of the tomatoes. Flavouring can be adjusted to suit your taste. I have used wholesome and pure ingredients throughout: butter rather than margarine, honey rather than sugar, sea salt instead of processed salt, brown flour instead of white – and always natural herb flavourings.

1

My thanks go to all who consumed with relish the dishes prepared in our kitchen and who baked and cooked with me. I bless Rosemary Miller for typing the well-worked pages, and my editor, Alison Lowry, for putting it all together.

May this book change your eating habits and bring you to the peak of health.

Herbs used in Cooking

BALM *(Melissa officinalis)*

Also known as lemon mint: Used in sweet dishes and in hot drinks. Lemon flavouring.

BASIL *(Ocimum basilicum)*

Basil is one of the most useful herbs in cooking. It has a rich, pungent flavour and, for its best full taste, is used fresh from the garden. It can be used dried but a lot of flavour is lost in the drying. Basil is delicious in tomato dishes, pasta dishes and sauces.

BAY *(Laurus nobilis)*

Also known as bay laurel or sweet bay. Used for flavouring. A single leaf is strong enough to flavour an average stew. Remove after cooking. Bay leaves are an essential part of bouquet garni, and can also, surprisingly, be used in sweet dishes.

BORAGE *(Borago officinalis)*

Light cucumber flavour. Use the young leaves with fish, salads and particularly with potato and cucumber dishes. Add the flowers to mulled wine or cider.

BOUQUET GARNI

Classic bouquet garni is comprised of *bay leaf* and sprigs of *parsley, thyme* and *oreganum,* tied in a muslin bag – and then cooked in the dish and removed before serving. Other herbs may be added to this basic combination if desired.

BURNET (Salad Burnet) *(Sanguisorba officinalis)*

The flavour of salad burnet resembles cucumber and the stripped leaves are delicious in soups and stews, and in spiced vinegars and sauces.

CHERVIL *(Anthriscus cerefolium)*

Slight anise flavour. Needs to be added to the dish right at the end of the cooking time. Delicious in soups, stews and casseroles, egg, cheese and fish dishes, sauces and herb butters. This herb mixes well with other herbs as it has a bland flavour.

4

CELERY *(Apium graveolens)*

Celery is not often thought of as a herb, but it is an important one. It has a delicious meaty flavour and enhances savoury dishes. Use chopped leaves and stems in soups, stews and casseroles. Combines well with other herbs.

CHIVES *(Allium schoenoprasum)*

Mild onion flavour. Chives need to be used fresh, scissor-snipped, sprinkled on the dish, or mixed into cream cheese, omelettes and cheese dishes. Use the flowers to garnish.

COMFREY *(Symphytum officinale)*

Comfrey is a mild, bland herb and combines well with other herbs. Because of its wonderful medicinal properties it should be lavishly used in soups and stews. It dies down in winter but often a few new leaves can be found if you look carefully.

DILL *(Peucedanum graveolens)*

Slight anise flavour. Chopped leaves need to be added to a dish at the end of the cooking time. Dill is particularly good in fish dishes and vegetable dishes, especially with marrow, tomato and cabbage. Cooked with mushrooms, dill aids the digestion as well.

FENNEL *(Foeniculum vulgare)*

Stronger liquorice flavour than dill, fennel is even better in fish dishes and in sauces. Grill fish on a bed of fennel. Fennel also helps break down the oiliness of certain fish, making it more digestible.

FINES HERBES

This is a classic combination of four herbs: *chervil, chives, parsley* and *tarragon*. Can be made from fresh or dried herbs, equal quantities of each. Use for fish, chicken and vegetable dishes and sauces.

GARLIC *(Allium sativum)*

This is probably the strongest flavoured herb. It is used in many savoury dishes, sauces, vinegars, breads, marinades and herb butters. Can be used fresh or dried.
To remove the strong garlic smell from the breath, chew a sprig of parsley.

HORSE-RADISH *(Armoracia rusticana)*

This has a very hot, pungent flavour. The grated root is used fresh in sauces or pickled in vinegar. Delicious with fish, beef and beetroot.

LOVAGE *(Levisticum officinale)*

Of the celery family, lovage has a rich, strong, meaty flavour. It is used in rich gravies, stews, sauces and casseroles. It does not dry well, so use fresh lovage if possible.

MARJORAM *(Origanum onites)*

This herb has a pungent, spicy flavour and is particularly delicious with baked potatoes and in stews and omelettes. It can easily be dried and it stores well, although fresh, green marjoram is using it at its best. Sprinkle over roasting chicken and duck.

MINTS *(Mentha* varieties)

Mints are used in sauces or added, chopped, to either sweet or savoury dishes. Delicious in teas and hot, spiced drinks. Mint makes all the difference to carrot dishes, peas and dried beans. Use peppermint in teas and hot puddings.

OREGANO *(Origanum vulgare)*

Related to marjoram, it is stronger in flavour and needs to be used sparingly. It is at its best in pasta dishes and tomato sauces. Needs to be used on its own as it is so strong.

PARSLEY *(Petroselinum crispum)*

This is the most versatile of all herbs. It is well known as a garnish. Use lavishly in all savoury dishes and combine with other herbs as it is an excellent mixer.

ROSEMARY *(Rosmarinus officinalis)*

Dominant and strong, rosemary needs to be used on its own. Use sparingly as it has a distinctive flavour. Delicious in marinades and sweet dishes, as well as cooked with old favourites like lamb and chicken. Try roasting lamb on a bed of fresh rosemary sprigs. Use finely minced in scones and tarts, stuffings and breads.

SAGE *(Salvia officinalis)*

Sage is slightly bitter, strong and very distinctive. It does not combine easily with other herbs and very little is needed to give a strong flavour. Use fresh or dried. Good with poultry, pulses and certain vegetables like eggfruit, peas, sweet potatoes and tomatoes.

SAVORY *(Satureja montana)*

The perennial winter savory has a peppery, pungent taste and a little goes a long way. Particularly in marinades and in soups and stews, winter savory combines well with other herbs. Use finely chopped in pastry, in meat loaves and breads and with broad beans and beetroot.

SCENTED GERANIUM *(Pelargonium graveolens)*

Although frost sensitive, if protected through the winter, scented geraniums will yield some fragrant leaves for flavouring cakes and puddings, particularly rice and sago puddings. Use fresh and green.

SORREL *(Rumex acetosa)*

Acid in flavour, sorrel dies down somewhat in winter but the new leaves shoot up constantly and can be added to soups and stews. Sorrel combines well with other herbs.

TARRAGON *(Artemisia dracunculoides)*

Use chopped tarragon in egg and fish dishes. Particularly good with mushrooms, cabbage and beetroot, tarragon combines pleasantly with all herbs as it is mild in taste.

THYME *(Thymus vulgaris)*

Common thyme has a distinctive flavour and this is probably one of the most versatile of culinary herbs. Excellent in most savoury dishes, vegetable dishes, and baked into breads and scones, thyme is a favourite herb with which to experiment. It does not combine well with other herbs, however, so use it on its own.

LEMON THYME *(Thymus citriodorus)*

Distinctly lemon-flavoured and scented. Can be used in steamed or baked puddings, cakes and sweet tarts, jams and jellies.

WATERCRESS *(Nasturtium officinale)*

Peppery and stimulating, watercress can be used in soups, stews and chopped into batters and sauces. It combines well with other herbs.

The above list is made up of fairly common and well-known herbs, but this should not limit you in your cookery. You should always search for and experiment with the unusual – for the unusual lends excitement. I have chosen those herbs most easily available to all housewives and cooks. These can either be grown in the garden or in pots on a balcony. No cook need ever be without fresh herbs on hand.

Many of the herbs can be dried but in my cookery classes and in my own kitchen I always prefer to use freshly picked herbs from the garden. When substituting dried herbs for fresh ones, usually halve the quantity, for example

2 tsp (10 ml) fresh marjoram equals
1 tsp (5 ml) dried marjoram.

Soups

Winter soup served for dinner, supper or lunch is warming, filling and comforting. It is an essential part of winter cooking and, using only a few basic recipes, many changes and variations can be made to satisfy the most difficult and finicky of eaters. Since most soups require prolonged boiling, herbs can be added during the last few minutes so as to ensure their perfect flavour is at its richest, or chopped and stirred in at the very last moment. Used in this way the most delicate of herbs retains its flavour and goodness and the stronger flavoured herbs are not allowed to dominate the dish.

Another way to flavour soups or sauces is to infuse the herb. Pour boiling water over the herb, steep for 30 minutes, strain and then use the liquid as a base for a soup.

GENERAL QUANTITIES FOR HERB STOCK

1 cup herbs (eg tarragon, lovage, celery, chervil, chives, parsley),
  chopped and well pressed into the cup
6–10 cups boiling water

Add a little of the same herb, freshly chopped, to garnish at serving time.

BASIC STOCK   Makes 2-3 litres (4-6 pt)

All good soups require a rich basic stock and this can be inexpensively made quickly and easily. Save your vegetable peelings and store in a plastic bag in the fridge.

Wash carrot peelings and a few carrot leaves
Wash potato peelings
Add a few celery leaves, parsley stalks, sticks of cauliflower
  etc.

This quantity should equal 4-6 cups, well pressed down.

1 chicken carcass, chicken skin, bones or
3-6 soup bones or
Sunday roast bones

14

Boil up in 2-3 litres (4-6 pt) water for 20-30 minutes in a covered pot. Strain and use this liquid as your soup base.

CARROT AND CELERY SOUP (Serves 6-8)

225 g (8 oz) grated carrots
225 g (8 oz) grated turnips
40 g (3 tbsp) butter
1 large onion, chopped
500 ml (2 cups) celery leaves and stalks, chopped
sea salt and black pepper to taste
1 litre (1¾ pt) chicken stock

Fry the onion in the butter for 5 minutes. Stir in and lightly fry carrots, then turnips. Add all other ingredients, except the celery. Simmer for 30 minutes in a covered pot. Lastly add celery and stand for 5 minutes or mix in a liquidiser for 2 minutes. Serve garnished with a sprig of celery or a little chopped celery – or serve straight from the pot with a little chopped celery for decoration.

RICH WINTER VEGETABLE SOUP (Serves 6-10)

225 g (8 oz) grated fresh carrots
225 g (8 oz) grated fresh potatoes
225 g (8 oz) finely chopped fresh green outer leaves of cabbage
2 large onions, finely chopped
2 large leeks, finely chopped
3-4 large tomatoes, finely chopped
250 ml (1 cup) pearl barley that has been soaked in water overnight
250 ml (1 cup) haricot or butter beans that have been soaked in water overnight
2–3 litres (3½–4½ pt) chicken stock
sea salt and black pepper to taste
250 ml (1 cup) comfrey leaves, chopped
250 ml (1 cup) borage leaves, chopped
½ cup chopped parsley
40 g (1½ oz or 3 tbsp) butter

Fry onions and leeks in butter for 5 minutes. Add and stir-fry the carrots for 5 minutes. Add all other ingredients and the water in which the barley and the beans have been soaked. Simmer for 40 minutes or until the beans are tender. Taste and add a little marmite if desired. Serve with croûtons and chopped fresh parsley sprinkled on top.

CAULIFLOWER AND MUSHROOM SOUP (Serves 6-8)

1 medium head cauliflower
40 g (1 ½ oz or 3 tbsp) butter
1 litre (1¾ pt) stock
1 litre (1¾ pt) milk
225 g (8 oz) mushrooms, fresh, washed and thinly sliced
50 ml (4 tbsp) cream
sea salt, pepper to taste
250 ml (1 cup) chopped, fresh tarragon

Chop cauliflower and stir-fry in butter for 5 minutes. Add all ingredients except tarragon and cream. Simmer for 30 minutes. Pour into a liquidiser and purée for 3 minutes. Return to the pan, reheat, stir in cream and tarragon and serve immediately.

BEETROOT AND SAGE SOUP (Serves 6-10)

675 g – 1 kg (2-3 lb) raw beetroots
2 litres (3½ pt) stock
40 g (3 tbsp) butter
2 large onions, finely chopped
500 ml (2 cups) kidney beans, soaked overnight in water
250 ml (1 cup) cream
sea salt, black pepper to taste
125-250 ml (½-1 cup) brown sugar
*125-190 ml (½-¾ cup) finely chopped sage or fresh sage tied up
  in cheesecloth*

Fry onions in the butter for 5 minutes. Peel beetroot, and top and tail, and grate raw on a coarse grater. Add all ingredients except cream and sage. Simmer for 30-40 minutes or until beans are tender. Add sage in the last 5-8 minutes of cooking time. If using cheesecloth method, simmer in the soup for the last 5 minutes, removing before serving. Purée in liquidiser for 3 minutes. Return to pot, reheat and stir in cream. Serve hot with a little fresh sage sprinkled on top.

PUMPKIN AND BASIL SOUP (Serves 6-8)

450 g (1 lb) pumpkin, chopped and peeled
225 g (8 oz) grated carrots
2 medium onions, finely chopped
900 ml (1½ pt) chicken stock
225 g (8 oz) tomatoes, chopped
40 g (3 tbsp) butter
sea salt, pepper to taste
125 ml (½ cup) brown sugar
37,5-50 ml (3-4 tbsp) thick cream
37,5 ml (3 tbsp) chopped basil

Fry chopped onion in the butter for 5 minutes. Stir-fry the carrots, add pumpkin and chopped tomatoes and a little stock. Cook briskly until soft. Put through a liquidiser with a little of the stock if needed. Return to pot and add all ingredients except the basil and simmer for about 10 minutes. In the last few minutes of cooking stir in the basil and serve immediately.

HERBED LENTIL AND SPLIT PEA SOUP (Serves 6–8)

100 g (4 oz) lentils (brown), soaked in water overnight
100 g (4 oz) split peas, soaked in water overnight
2 medium onions, finely chopped
37,5-50 ml (3-4 tbsp) maize oil
100 g (4 oz) chopped spinach
50 g (2 oz) chopped celery
50 g (2 oz) chopped parsley
25 g (1 oz) chopped rosemary
juice of 1 lemon
sea salt, pepper to taste
150 ml (¼ pt) yoghurt or buttermilk
1,2 litres (2 pt) chicken stock

Fry chopped onions in the oil for 5 minutes. Stir-fry chopped spinach. Add all other ingredients except the yoghurt or buttermilk and parsley. Simmer for 20 minutes. Purée in a liquidiser for 2 minutes, return to the pot, reheat and stir in the yoghurt or buttermilk and parsley. Serve hot with croûtons.

Fish Dishes

Several herbs enhance fish dishes and, whether cooked with the fish or chopped into a sauce, the herbs will help in digesting the fish and will dissolve any fattiness.

GRILLED FISH WITH HERB SAUCE (Serves 4)

450 g (1 lb) fish
juice of 1 lemon
sea salt, freshly ground black pepper to taste
25 ml (2 tbsp) chopped fennel leaves
12,5 ml (1 tbsp) flour
30 g (2.tbsp) butter
12,5 ml (1 tbsp) dry mustard
25 ml (2 tbsp) celery leaves, chopped
25 ml (2 tbsp) chopped parsley
250 ml (8 fluid oz) milk

Melt half the butter in a pan, add chopped herbs, stir, and add flour. Add milk, into which the mustard has been blended, and mix well until it starts to thicken. Place trimmed, cleaned fish pieces in an ovenproof dish, dot with butter, and sprinkle with lemon juice, salt and pepper. Place under the grill and cook for 5 minutes on each side or until fish is cooked. Pour the herb and mustard sauce over the grilled fish and place under the grill for 3–5 minutes. Serve with a green salad.

PARSLEY CHOWDER (Serves 6-8)

This is a rich, warming fish casserole or soup. It is a perfect meal on its own and needs only home-made brown bread to make it complete.

30 g (2 tbsp) butter
675 g (1½ lb) fish
450 g (1 lb) potatoes
sea salt, black pepper to taste
300 ml (½ pt) cream
2 medium onions, finely chopped
75 ml (6 tbsp) chopped parsley
50 ml (4 tbsp) chopped dill leaves
few sprigs watercress, if available
hot water or stock

Choose a large heavy pan with a lid. Heat the butter and fry the chopped onion in it. Add the fish pieces and coat with butter. Peel and slice the potatoes 0,5 cm (¼") thick and add to the casserole. Sprinkle with salt and pepper. Add enough hot water or stock to just cover the potatoes and fish. Bring to the boil, then simmer for 30 minutes in the covered pan. Add the cream, stirring slowly, but do not break up the potatoes. Add the herbs and serve in soup bowls.

TROUT WITH HERB STUFFING (Serves 6)

6 trout
juice of 2 lemons
37,5 ml (3 tbsp) chopped basil
37,5 ml (3 tbsp) chopped parsley
40 g (3 tbsp) butter
salt and pepper
10 ml (2 tsp) Tabasco or Worcestershire sauce
37,5 ml (3 tbsp) fresh breadcrumbs

Wash and trim trout and remove heads and tails. Make three diagonal slits on each side of the trout. Fill the cleaned cavities with the mixed butter, herbs, sauce and breadcrumbs. Place the fish in a buttered casserole. Sprinkle with salt and pepper and lemon juice, push any leftover stuffing among the fish, dot with butter, cover with a lid or tinfoil and bake for 20–30 minutes at medium heat. Remove lid for last five minutes to brown the fish slightly. Serve with fresh lemon wedges.

FRIED FISH WITH HERBS (Serves 6)

675 g (1½ lb) fish

Batter
1 egg, beaten
250 ml (1 cup) flour
salt and black pepper to taste
25 ml (2 tbsp) chopped sage
little milk
1 clove garlic, finely minced

Blend batter ingredients. Pour over each piece of fish, coating well. Fry fish in the hot oil for 3-5 minutes. (I find it easier to use a frying basket, placing several pieces of fish in the basket at once. There is no need to turn the fish.) Remove from the oil, then recoat with batter and fry for a further 3–5 minutes or until the fish is cooked. Drain on crumpled brown paper. Keep hot in the oven. In the same oil fry some sliced potatoes (4 medium potatoes) and serve sprinkled with a little salt, pepper and chopped sage.

BAKED FISH WITH ROSEMARY (Serves 6)

575 g (1¼ lb) fish, divided into 6 portions
juice of 2 lemons
1 clove garlic, finely minced
250 ml (1 cup) chopped onions
4 large tomatoes, skinned and sliced
sprigs fresh rosemary
salt and black pepper to taste
2 tbsp butter
2 tbsp fresh chopped rosemary
pieces of tinfoil

23

Brush six pieces of tinfoil with oil. Sprinkle fish portions with salt and pepper and place on the oiled tinfoil on top of a sprig of rosemary. Sprinkle the chopped onions, tomatoes, garlic and a little chopped rosemary over the fish. Dot with butter and squeeze a little lemon juice over it all. Fold up the edges of the tinfoil. Place in a baking tray and bake at 180°C (350°F) for 25 minutes. Serve with mashed potatoes.

Meat Dishes

To all meat dishes herbs impart a full flavour and once you begin to experiment with herbs in different combinations you will be thrilled with the results. Be bold and try out unusual herbs. The recipes below are starting points; each dish can vary according to your own taste. Throughout this book I have used quick and easy recipes for busy people, and no less so in this section.

HERBED RISSOLES (Serves 6–8)

500 g (1¼ lb) lean mince
2 medium onions, finely chopped
25 ml (2 tbsp) chopped parsley
10-15 ml (2-3 tsp) fresh thyme
salt and pepper to taste
2 medium tomatoes, skinned and chopped
3 medium carrots, finely grated
37,5 ml (3 tbsp) chopped celery leaves and stalks
12,5 ml (1 tbsp) finely chopped lovage (if you have no lovage, use more celery)
2 eggs, beaten
oil
juice of 1 lemon

In a large mixing bowl mix together all the ingredients. Heat the oil in a pan (I usually have two pans going at the same time to speed up the cooking). Mould flat balls or cakes of the mixture in your hands and place the rissoles in the hot oil.
Turn to medium heat. When they start to brown turn them over and fry on the other side (usually 5-8 minutes on each side) until cooked. Drain on crumpled brown paper. Keep hot in the oven until ready to serve.

A *tomato sauce* can be made to serve with the rissoles.

3 large tomatoes, skinned and chopped
2 onions, finely chopped
4-6 basil leaves, finely chopped
125 ml (½ cup) brown sugar

Cook together until soft (about 6 minutes). Pour over the rissoles and serve on a bed of mashed potato.

WINTER STEW (Serves up to 10)

1 kg (3 lb) rump steak, diced
4 onions, sliced and chopped
4 large tomatoes, skinned and chopped
6 carrots, peeled and diced
4 potatoes, peeled and diced
10 dried apricots, soaked in water overnight
salt and pepper to taste
125 ml (½ cup) maize oil
125 ml (½ cup) flour
12,5 ml (1 tbsp) fresh oregano
25-37,5 ml (2-3 tbsp) chopped borage
little water (approx 2 cups)
10 ml (2 tsp) freshly ground coriander
bouquet garni

Sprinkle the diced meat with the flour, salt, pepper and coriander. Heat the oil in a large heavy-bottomed pot and brown the meat, turning quickly. Add onions and tomatoes and cook on low heat until softened. Then add the potatoes and carrots, apricots and the bouquet garni and the water. Stir carefully and cook on low heat for about 2 hours. Should it cook dry add a little more water and stir to prevent burning. Add oregano and borage just before serving. Remove bouquet garni. Serve with brown rice.

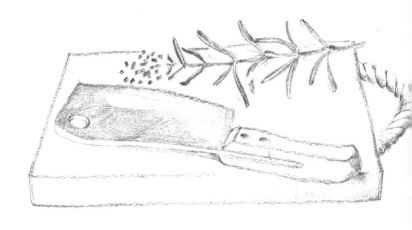

MARJORAM MEAT LOAF (Serves up to 10)

1½ kg (3 lb) lean mince
4 medium tomatoes, skinned and chopped
2 large onions, chopped
4 carrots, peeled and finely grated
4 comfrey leaves, chopped
25 ml (2 tbsp) marjoram
2 large eggs, beaten
1 garlic clove, minced
sea salt and black pepper to taste
6 bay leaves
6 potatoes, peeled and halved
125-190 ml (½-¾ cup) maize oil

In a large bowl mix all the ingredients except the bay leaves,
the potatoes and the oil. Form into a large loaf and place in a
roasting pan. Into the top of the loaf tuck the 6 bay leaves,
spacing evenly. Place the potatoes along the sides and pour the
oil over the meat loaf and potatoes. Bake in a medium oven
(180°C/350°F) for approximately one hour, basting with the oil
from time to time. Remove bay leaves before serving.

MUTTON HOT-POT (Serves up to 10)

1½ kg (3 lb) stewing mutton, or small loin chops
3 medium onions, finely chopped
250 ml (1 cup) chopped chives
500 g (½ lb) dried peaches
4-6 large potatoes, peeled and quartered
6 large carrots, peeled and diced
1 small cabbage, roughly chopped – remove the thick white
  midribs of the leaves
1-1½ litres (4-6 cups) stock
bouquet garni
20 ml (4 tsp) winter savory
5 ml (1 tsp) ground coriander
125 ml (½ cup) maize oil
125 ml (½ cup) flour
sea salt and black pepper to taste
125 ml (½ cup) honey

Heat oil in a large heavy-bottomed pot. Dice the mutton or trim the loin chops. Dip into seasoned flour and fry in the oil until browned. In the meantime prepare all the other ingredients and add to the browned mutton, all except the winter savory. Cover and simmer on low heat for approximately one hour. Stir occasionally and check that it does not become too dry. In the last 10 minutes of cooking add the winter savory. Remove bouquet garni and serve with brown rice and mint sauce.

Mint Sauce

125-190 ml (½-¾ cup) chopped mint
250 ml (1 cup) hot water
125 ml (½ cup) brown sugar
125 ml (½ cup) vinegar

Mix well, place in a screw-top bottle and shake. Pour a little sauce over the mutton hot-pot at the table.

· 29

PORK AND BEANS WINTER WARMER (Serves up to 10)

1½ kg (3 lb) lean pork chops
500 g (1 lb) kidney beans, soaked overnight and then boiled in
*   water for ½ hour*
4 large tomatoes, skinned and chopped
250 ml (1 cup) honey
250 ml (1 cup) chopped tarragon
125 ml (½ cup) chopped sage
500 g (1 lb) lean bacon, chopped
3 medium onions, chopped
1-1½ litres (4-6 cups) vegetable stock
bouquet garni
37,5 ml (3 tbsp) Torula debittered yeast
salt and black pepper to taste

Using a heavy-bottomed large pot, heat a little maize oil. Trim the chops of fat and brown for a few minutes. Add bacon and brown. Then add tomatoes and onions and stir until slightly cooked. Add beans, debittered yeast that has been mixed with a little water, bouquet garni, honey, salt, pepper and half the vegetable stock. Stir well, turn to low heat and simmer for one hour. Stir every now and again, adding a little more of the vegetable stock. In the last 10 minutes of cooking time add the sage and tarragon and stir in well. Serve with crusty bread and sauerkraut.

ROAST LAMB WITH HERB CRUST (Serves 4-8)

1 shoulder of lamb or *1 leg of lamb*

Place the lamb on a rack in a roasting pan and sprinkle with a little salt, pepper and fresh lemon juice. Roast in a medium oven (180°C/350°F) for 25 minutes per 0,5 kg (1 lb) in weight. Baste with the juices and a little maize oil, or olive oil, from time to time.

Herb Crust

While the lamb is roasting make a herb crust:

75 ml (6 tbsp) soft wholewheat breadcrumbs
25 ml (2 tbsp) chopped parsley
25 ml (2 tbsp) chopped mint
37,5 ml (3 tbsp) vinegar
25 ml (2 tbsp) finely chopped rosemary
25 ml (2 tbsp) maize oil
1 clove garlic, finely minced
salt and pepper to taste

Mix all ingredients together to form a paste. Twenty minutes before the roasting time is up, take the lamb out of the oven and spread the paste over the top surface of the lamb, pressing well down with a palette knife. Baste once with the pan juices and return to the oven to finish cooking. The crust should be golden brown once the cooking time is up.

I usually place potatoes around the meat and roast them at the same time, basting them with the pan juices as well as the bits and pieces of the herb crust that fall into the pan. This makes a delicious meal, served with gravy made from the pan juices in the following way. Remove the meat and potatoes, stir a little flour or gravy powder into the pan juices, add a cup or two of vegetable stock, stir well and pour into a gravy boat. Mint sauce, for those who enjoy the traditional roast lamb, is the usual accompaniment.

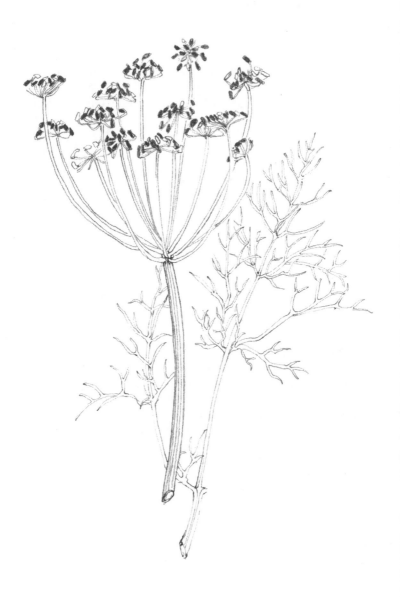

*Poultry
Dishes*

Chicken is one of the easiest and cheapest dishes to prepare and is a universal favourite. The recipes below can be adapted for duck, turkey or even goose. Always save the carcasses for stock and soups. Don't be afraid to experiment with different herbs to give your dishes a new taste and adapt the recipes as the mood or occasion takes you.

HERBED CHICKEN PANCAKES (Serves up to 8)

1,5 kg (3 lb) roasting chicken
juice of 1 lemon
1 onion
1 carrot
bouquet garni
1 stick celery
3-4 stalks parsley
salt and pepper to taste

Place the chicken in a large casserole on top of the stove and tuck the carrot, celery, onion and bouquet garni around it. Sprinkle with salt, pepper and lemon juice. Fill the casserole with enough cold water to reach halfway up the chicken. Bring to the boil and simmer gently for ¾ hour or until the chicken is tender. Then lift it out, drain and cool. Save the stock. Cut off the chicken meat into neat pieces, discarding bits of skin.

Batter

175 g (6 oz) wholewheat flour
pinch sea salt
2 eggs, beaten
250-300 ml (8-10 fluid oz) milk
25 ml (2 tbsp) finely chopped chervil
25 ml (2 tbsp) finely chopped fennel

Blend eggs into the milk. Place flour in a bowl, make a well in the centre and gradually pour in the milk and egg mixture. Add salt and herbs and beat well with a wooden spoon. Stand for one hour. The batter should have the consistency of heavy cream. Add a little more milk if necessary.

Chicken Filling

50 g (2 oz) butter
40 ml (3½ tbsp) flour
150 ml (¼ pt) thin cream
little salt and pepper
25 ml (2 tbsp) chopped chervil
50 g (2 oz) grated cheddar cheese
450 ml (¾ pt) chicken stock

Melt butter in a pan, stir in flour and cook for one minute, stirring all the time. Add the stock slowly, stirring constantly to blend well. As it starts to thicken, add cream, herbs and a little salt and pepper. Stir until it thickens. Reserve half the sauce and mix the remaining half with the chicken pieces.

Heat a little oil in a pan and make 10-12 pancakes with the batter. Divide the chicken filling among the pancakes and roll up into cigar shapes. Place in a baking dish, side by side, pour over the remaining sauce, sprinkle with the grated cheese and bake for 10 minutes in a medium oven (180°C/350°F) or until the top has browned.

This pancake batter can be used for any poultry or leftover cold chicken or meat. Vary the herbs to suit your taste.

Serve as a main dish with vegetables.

CHICKEN AND ASPARAGUS BAKE (Serves up to 10)

1 large chicken
1 carrot
1 onion
4 sprigs winter savory
1 large tin asparagus pieces

Boil the chicken in water in a heavy-bottomed pot with the winter savory, carrot and onion. Simmer for ¾ hour on low heat. Drain chicken, and save the stock. Cut chicken into bite-sized pieces and lay them in a large baking dish.

Drain the asparagus, saving the liquid. Lay the asparagus pieces over the chicken pieces in the baking dish.

Sauce

37,5 ml (3 tbsp) flour
25 ml (2 tbsp) butter
2 medium onions, chopped
250 ml (1 cup) stock
250 ml (1 cup) milk
250 ml (1 cup) asparagus liquid
250 ml (1 cup) cheese, grated
250 ml (1 cup) salad burnet leaves

Fry chopped onions in the butter in a medium sized pot. Add flour and stir well. Gradually add the chicken stock, the asparagus liquid and the milk. Stir in half the cheddar cheese as the sauce thickens. Lastly stir in salad burnet leaves and salt and pepper to taste. Pour the sauce over the chicken and asparagus and top with the rest of the grated cheese. Bake in a medium oven (180°C/350°F) for 20 minutes or until brown and bubbly. Serve with brown rice.

HERBED CHICKEN IN TERRACOTTA (Serves up to 8)

Unglazed clay pots are available almost anywhere today. They are foolproof to use and give baked chicken a most delicious flavour. Chicken cooked in this way is not only quick and easy but healthy as well as it cooks in only the natural flavours of herbs and its own juices. Remember to soak the terracotta casserole in cold water for 20 minutes before using it.

1 large chicken
3 sprigs thyme (stripped to make 2 teaspoons)
2 medium onions, finely chopped
1 clove garlic, finely chopped
125 ml (½ cup) chopped chives
3 sprigs parsley
1 thick slice wholewheat bread, crumbed
125 ml (½ cup) yoghurt or sour cream
salt and pepper to taste
juice of 1 lemon

Wash the chicken and remove giblets from the stomach cavity. Make a stuffing by combining the crumbed bread, chives, onions, chopped garlic, thyme, yoghurt or sour cream, the salt and pepper and a little of the lemon juice. Stuff the chicken with the mixture and place it on a bed of 4-6 thyme sprigs. Add 250-500 ml (1-2 cups) water. Slice an onion and place the pieces round the chicken. Sprinkle with salt, pepper and lemon juice, cover, and roast in a medium to hot oven for approximately 1-1½ hours. After one hour open the terracotta baking pot and check if the chicken is dry and done. Add a little water if necessary. Replace if it is now brown and succulent and cook for another few minutes.

I bake potatoes at the same time in the same oven alongside the terracotta pot, by merely placing washed potatoes (unpeeled) on the oven rack. They usually take ½-¾ hour. When they are baked, split them open and put a blob of butter and a sprinkling of chopped chives into each one.

CHICKEN SMOTHERED IN HERBS (Serves up to 8)

1 large chicken
250 ml (1 cup) chopped celery or lovage
125 ml (½ cup) chopped oregano
125 ml (½ cup) chopped parsley
125 ml (½ cup) chopped mint
2-4 bay leaves
250 ml (1 cup) chopped chives
1 clove garlic, finely chopped
125-190 ml (½-¾ cup) thick cream
squeeze of lemon juice
salt and pepper to taste

Cut one large piece heavy duty tinfoil. Wash and trim the chicken, remove giblets, and place chicken on the tinfoil. Mix all the chopped herbs, except the bay leaves, with the cream, salt and pepper.

Stuff the chicken with most of this mixture, saving some for placing around the chicken. Squeeze the lemon juice over the chicken and sprinkle with salt and pepper. Place the bay leaves around and on top. Fold up the tinfoil, making a neat parcel. Place chicken on a baking sheet or into a roasting pan. Roast in a medium oven (180°C/350°F) for approximately one hour or until the chicken is brown and succulent. Open the tinfoil parcel and save all the juices for gravy. Serve with brown rice.

MARINADED CHICKEN CASSEROLE (Serves up to 10)

10 chicken pieces
500 ml (2 cups) marinade
250 g (8 oz) mushrooms
125 ml (½ cup) chopped sage
125 ml (½ cup) chopped celery or lovage
250 ml (1 cup) smooth apricot jam
250 ml (1 cup) flour
salt and pepper to taste

Marinate the chicken overnight in the sauce. Next morning·
dip each piece of chicken into the flour, sprinkle with a little
salt and pepper and place in a casserole dish. Strain the remaining marinade and pour over the chicken pieces. Tuck the
chopped herbs in around the chicken. Wash and slice the
mushrooms, placing them on top of and around the chicken
pieces and spoon over the apricot jam. Cover with a lid or with
tinfoil. Bake in a medium oven (180°C/350°F) for 1½ hours.
Check from time to time to see that it is not drying out (add a
little water if it seems too dry) and when the chicken is tender
remove from the oven and serve with brown rice or mashed
potatoes.

Vegetable
Dishes

For today's housewife, stretching her housekeeping budget, meat and poultry dishes are expensive, and her ingenuity at turning ordinary vegetables into satisfying and sustaining meals is tried to the utmost. Costwise, vegetables are far cheaper than meat and their nutritional content is excellent. These dishes can be substituted for meat dishes for vegetarians and they lend themselves with relish to our winter diets.

LENTIL CURRY WITH BASIL (Serves up to 6)

2 large onions, chopped finely
4 stalks celery, chopped (leaves as well)
25 ml (2 tbsp) chopped basil
10 ml (2 tsp) curry powder
5 ml (1 tsp) turmeric
2 ml (½ tsp) cumin
375 ml (1½ cups) brown lentils, soaked one hour in boiling water
125 ml (½ cup) chopped parsley
900 ml (4½ cups) water
4 cups chopped, shredded cabbage
50 ml (4 tbsp) brown sugar
1 grated apple
4 large tomatoes, skinned and chopped
2-5 ml (½-1 tsp) salt
pepper to taste
200 ml (¾ cup) sour cream
125 ml (½ cup) pineapple jam
25 ml (2 tbsp) butter

Over medium heat, brown the onions in the butter. Add tomatoes, celery and basil. Cook until soft. Add cabbage, apple and water and cook for 5 minutes, stirring all the time. Add salt, sugar, turmeric, cumin, and curry powder and mix well. Add lentils and mix well.

Turn into a buttered casserole, spoon over the sour cream, pineapple jam and parsley and cover with lid or tinfoil. Bake at 180°C (350°F) for 30-40 minutes. (Adjust curry powder to your taste – this amount is mild.)

BEAN STEW (Serves up to 10)

500 g (1 lb) butter beans
500 g (1 lb) kidney beans
250 ml (1 cup) split peas
500 ml (2 cups) diced potatoes
500 ml (2 cups) diced carrots
500 ml (2 cups) chopped onions
4 cups chopped tomatoes
2 cloves garlic, finely chopped
12,5 ml (1 tbsp) oreganum
6 ml (1/2 tbsp) thyme
2 bay leaves
125-250 ml (1/2-1 cup) maize oil
125 ml (1/2 cup) Worcestershire sauce
salt and pepper to taste
37,5–50 ml (3-4 tbsp) honey

Soak beans and peas overnight in enough water to cover them.
In the morning drain and wash in fresh water, place in a large,
heavy-bottomed pot, cover with water, add the bay leaves and
boil up for one hour. Remove bay leaves and drain. Fry
onions, carrots and potatoes in the oil until lightly browned.
Add all the other ingredients and the beans. The split peas will
have become mushy but this adds to the rich consistency of the
pot. (You may prefer to add the soaked split peas at this point.)
Cook slowly over a low heat for 30-40 minutes or until beans
are tender. At the end of the cooking time stir in honey and a
little fresh oreganum. Should the stew become dry at any point
add a little tomato juice or water to keep it succulent. This is a
very satisfying meal and needs only to be served with crusty
bread to make it perfect.

SAUERKRAUT (Serves 6-10)

1 red cabbage, shredded, ribs removed
1 drumhead cabbage, shredded, ribs removed
4 grated apples
1 cup seedless raisins
500 ml (2 cups) vinegar
125 ml (½ cup) brown sugar
500 ml (2 cups) water
6 ml (½ tbsp) caraway seeds
125-250 ml (½-1 cup) chopped sorrel leaves, if available
125-250 ml (½-1 cup) chopped comfrey leaves, if available
pinch salt
black pepper

Place cabbages in a large, heavy-bottomed pot and add the
other ingredients. Boil up slowly and simmer for 30-40 minutes in a covered pot until the cabbage is tender. Add sorrel
and comfrey leaves. Drain off the vinegar and water and turn
the cabbage into a serving dish. Dot with butter and add
freshly ground black pepper and a little salt. Serve with hardboiled eggs and grated cheese.

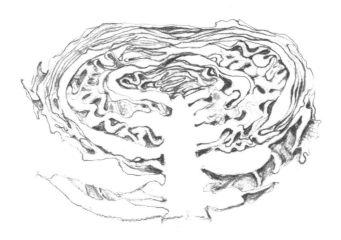

BROAD BEANS WITH HERB SAUCE (Serves 4–6)

Broad beans are easy to grow in the winter garden and are rich in protein and minerals.

1,25 kg (2½ lb) broad beans which equals
350–400 g (14 oz–1lb) podded beans

Sauce

15 g (½ oz) butter
15 g (½ oz) flour
150 ml (¼ pt) milk
12,5 ml (1 tbsp) chopped parsley
25 ml (2 tbsp) salad burnet, stripped and chopped
12,5 ml (1 tbsp) chopped mint
12,5 ml (1 tbsp) cream
salt and pepper to taste

Boil the beans in water, to which a few sprigs of mint have been added, for about 15 minutes or until tender. While they are boiling make the sauce. Melt the butter, stir in the flour, salt and pepper, and add the milk slowly, stirring all the time with a wire whisk. Boil for 2-3 minutes, remove from heat, and stir in cream and chopped herbs.

Mix in the beans and top with 125 ml (½ cup) grated cheese. Brown briefly under the grill before serving.

PUMPKIN PIE (Serves up to 12)

Pastry Shell

500 ml (2 cups) wholewheat flour
520 ml (1 cup) butter
2 ml (½ tsp) salt
⅓-½ cup iced water

Mix salt into the flour. Work in butter with fingers until it resembles breadcrumbs. Stir in the iced water with a fork until it forms a fairly stiff dough. Wrap the dough in greased paper and place in the refrigerator while you prepare the filling. This is a plain basic pastry shell that can be used for any fillings, savoury or sweet.

Filling

3 cups pumpkin, cooked and mashed
250-375 ml (1-1½ cups) brown sugar
25 ml (2 tbsp) molasses or honey
2 ml (½ tsp) powdered cloves
15 ml (3 tsp) cinnamon (powdered)
15 ml (3 tsp) ginger (powdered)
5 ml (1 tsp) salt
4 eggs, slightly beaten
500 ml (2 cups) hot milk

Mix the ingredients, in the order given, into the cooked, mashed pumpkin with a fork.

Line two 23 cm (9″) pie plates with the thinly rolled out pastry, fork the edges or pinch and fill with the pumpkin mixture. Take thin strips of left-over pastry and crisscross over the pie – or roll out a thin top, prick and seal. Bake in a medium oven at 180°C (350°F) for approximately 40 minutes or until the pie is browned and the under crust cooked through. This can be dusted with sugar and cinnamon if it is to be served as a sweet dish, or served plain as a savoury vegetable dish with a stew or roast.

WINTER VEGETABLE HOT POT (Serves up to 10)

6 carrots, peeled and diced
3 turnips, peeled and diced
1 small cauliflower, broken into florets
1 small cabbage, finely shredded and chopped
3 medium onions, finely chopped
3 medium potatoes, peeled and diced
1 litre (4 cups) stock
3 bay leaves
12,5 ml (1 tbsp) salt
pepper to taste
12,5-37,5 ml (1–3 tbsp) honey
12,5 ml (1 tbsp) thyme
250 ml (1 cup) chopped celery leaves and stalks
125 ml (½ cup) parsley
250 ml (1 cup) cheddar cheese, grated

Boil up all the vegetables and ingredients in the stock on a medium heat, except the celery and parsley. Cook for about 30 minutes or until the vegetables are tender. Stir in the chopped celery and cook for five minutes. Strain, and pour the vegetables into a casserole, reserving the liquid for soup. Dot with butter, and sprinkle with parsley and cheese. Brown under the grill for 5 minutes. Serve with fingers of wholewheat marmite toast.

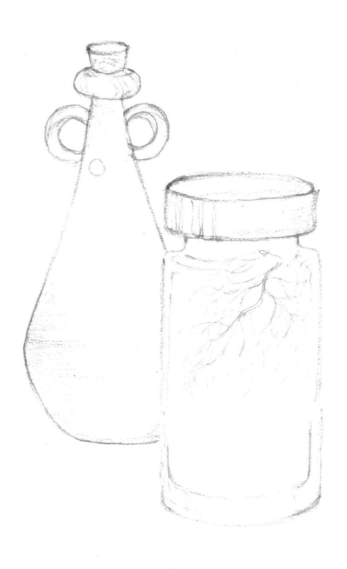

Vegetable and Herb Chart

A sprinkling of herbs can give vegetables a suble and different taste. Boil vegetables in your usual way. Drain, dot with butter, sprinkle with one or two different herbs and a little salt and pepper. The following combinations are delicious.

Beans (kidney, haricot, butter etc) – thyme, oregano, marjoram, rosemary
Beetroot – tarragon, sage, mint, horseradish
Broad beans – tarragon, sage, savory
Brussels sprouts – mint, thyme, chervil
Cabbage – parsley, tarragon, sage, fennel
Carrots – mint, comfrey, borage
Cauliflower – chervil, celery, lovage, dill, fennel
Fennel bulb – parsley, tarragon, dill
Kohlrabi – basil, thyme, sage
Onions – basil, rosemary, sage, celery
Parsnip – chervil, horseradish, sorrel
Potatoes – thyme, rosemary, marjoram, sorrel, celery, mint, oregano, lovage
Pumpkin – celery, fennel, dill, mint
Tomatoes – basil, tarragon, thyme, chervil, savory, sorrel
Turnips – horseradish, watercress, sorrel

Sauces and Accompaniments

Sauces can be served separately or poured over the finished dish. Often a plain dish can be made into something special with a tasty sauce accompaniment. Even plain rice or pasta or hardboiled eggs can become a treat served with one of the sauces below.

RICH TOMATO SAUCE WITH HERBS (Serves 6)

6-8 medium tomatoes, skinned and chopped
2 medium onions, finely chopped
12,5 ml (1 tbsp) thyme
25-50 ml (2-4 tbsp) sorrel, chopped
25-50 ml (2-4 tbsp) celery or lovage (or both)
180-250 ml (²/₃ - 1 cup) brown sugar
little salt, cayenne pepper
1 cup raisins, soaked in hot water for 10-15 minutes
125 ml (½ cup) oil (maize or sunflower)
125 ml (½ cup) vinegar
chopped parsley

Fry the onions and celery in the oil until they start to brown. Add the rest of the ingredients. Stir over medium heat until cooked – about 6-10 minutes. Pour over pasta, rice or shredded, cooked cabbage. Sprinkle with chopped parsley.

CHEESE SAUCE WITH HERBS (Serves 6)

37,5 ml (3 tbsp) butter
1 small onion, quartered
2 small diced carrots
1 stalk celery, diced
750 ml (3 cups) milk
chopped parsley
10 ml (2 tsp) fines herbes
2 bay leaves
salt
peppercorns
75 ml (6 tbsp) cake flour
125 ml (½ cup) cream (optional)
250-500 ml (1-2 cups) cheddar, grated

Boil up the milk with the carrots, onion and celery. Remove
from stove and allow to infuse. Add salt (about 5 ml (1 tsp)),
few peppercorns, and bay leaves. Stand for 30 minutes, stirring every now and then. Strain. In a heavy-bottomed pot melt
the butter and blend in the cake flour, stirring all the time with
a wooden spoon. Add the milk slowly until sauce thickens.
Bring to the boil, beat with an egg whisk, add fines herbes and
boil for 3 minutes. Add cream if desired. Remove from heat,
fold in the grated cheddar cheese and a little chopped parsley.
Serve over cauliflower, rice, pasta, toast or butter beans.

BASIL CREAM SAUCE (Serves 4-6)

(Substitute basil with lovage, tarragon, salad burnet, sorrel, watercress or borage.)

250 ml (1 cup) chives, chopped
1 medium onion, chopped
1 clove garlic, finely chopped
500 ml (2 cups) heavy cream
12,5-25 ml (1-2 tbsp) butter
250 ml (1 cup) chopped basil
12,5 ml (1 tbsp) flour

Fry the onion, chives and garlic in the butter until they start to brown. Add flour and stir. Pour in the cream and heat through. Stir in the basil and immediately serve over chicken breasts, butter beans, cabbage or mashed potatoes.

MARINADE

500 ml (2 cups) red wine
10 ml (2 tsp) mustard
125 ml (½ cup) honey
12,5-25 ml (1-2 tbsp) Worcestershire sauce
12,5 ml (1 tbsp) curry powder
12,5 ml (1 tbsp) fines herbes

Mix well, or shake all ingredients together in a screw-top jar. Use as a marinade for meat, poultry or fish.

HERBED VINEGAR SAUCE

1 litre (4 cups) brown grape vinegar
4 cups brown sugar
10 peppercorns
10 cloves
4 bay leaves
1 sprig rosemary
5 allspice berries
12,5 ml (1 tbsp) coriander seeds

Boil up herbs and spices in the vinegar. Simmer for 20 minutes in a covered pot. Stir in brown sugar. Remove from heat. Stand for one hour. Strain and bottle, placing a fresh rosemary sprig in the bottle. Use in gravies, add to meat loaves, tomato dishes, pickled fish, pickled pork etc. It keeps indefinitely. It is particularly good in lentil and bean dishes.

HORSERADISH SAUCE (1)

Winter is the time to dig up horseradish plants and grate the roots. Return the tops or bits of root to the soil for the next crop.

Finely grate enough horseradish roots to fill a jar. Cover with spiced vinegar (made by boiling one or two bay leaves, peppercorns, allspice berries and coriander in vinegar for 10-20 minutes). Seal and stand at least two weeks before use.

Use this horseradish in a white sauce to serve with vegetables like beetroot, turnip, cabbage and cauliflower.

HORSERADISH SAUCE (2)

500 ml (2 cups) milk
25 ml (2 tbsp) butter
25 ml (2 tbsp) flour or maizena
250 ml (1 cup) horseradish strained from the vinegar
12,5 ml (1 tbsp) sugar
little salt and pepper

Melt butter, stir in flour and add milk slowly, stirring all the time until sauce thickens. Add sugar, salt and pepper and horseradish. Blend. Serve with roasts – mutton or beef or chicken.

LONG-LIFE MINT SAUCE

This sauce will keep indefinitely and can be made at the end of summer while mint is abundant.

250 ml (1 cup) brown sugar
625 ml (2½ cups) white grape vinegar
500 ml (2 cups) chopped garden mint

Boil up vinegar and sugar for 3-5 minutes in a covered pot. Pour immediately over the mint and leave covered until cold. Pour into a jar, seal and keep in a dark cupboard. When needed, dilute 1 part mint sauce to 2 parts water. Mix well and serve separately with mutton dishes, bean dishes, etc.

Quick Suppers, Lunches and Snacks

PIZZA WITH HERBS (Makes two 23 cm/9" pizzas)

Crust

500 ml (2 cups) wholewheat flour
250 ml (1 cup) butter
5 ml (1 tsp) salt
10 ml (2 tsp) thyme
5 ml (1 tsp) baking powder
enough milk to make a fairly firm dough

Rub butter into the flour. Add salt, baking powder and thyme. Start with 125 ml (½ cup) milk, stir well, adding more milk to bind it into dough. On a floured board roll out dough thinly, and cut to fit two 23 cm (9") shallow pie plates or bake flat on a baking sheet.

Note: This is a quick and easy dough and not the standard pizza dough.

CONVENTIONAL PIZZA CRUST (Makes two 23 cm/9" pizzas)

12,5 ml (1 tbsp) dry active yeast
5 ml (1 tsp) sugar
60 ml (¼ cup) warm water
250 ml (1 cup) wholewheat flour
250 ml (1 cup) cake flour
160-190 ml (⅔-¾ cup) warm water
5 ml (1 tsp) salt
12,5-25 ml (1-2 tbsp) olive oil

In a small bowl dissolve yeast and sugar in the warm water. Allow to rise and become foamy. Mix the wholewheat and cake flours in a large bowl. Make a well in the centre and stir in the foamy yeast. Lightly mix in the surrounding flour and let it rise for about ten minutes. To this sponge gradually add the 160 ml (⅔ cup) warm water, olive oil and the salt. Knead on a floured board for 10 minutes. Place in a greased bowl. Cover with a clean towel, keep in a warm place and let it rise until it is double in size (45 minutes to 1½ hours). Then punch down and let it rest for 15 minutes. Form by hand into pizza rounds.

Herb Topping

4 large ripe tomatoes, skinned and chopped
250 g (8 oz) chopped, lean bacon
2 garlic cloves, minced
25 ml (2 tbsp) chopped basil
25 ml (2 tbsp) chopped chives
4 fresh sage sprigs
1 medium onion, chopped
25-37,5 ml (2-3 tbsp) olive oil
salt and freshly ground pepper
few olives and anchovies if desired
fresh chopped parsley
25 ml (2 tbsp) brown sugar
250 ml (1 cup) grated cheese – cheddar or parmesan

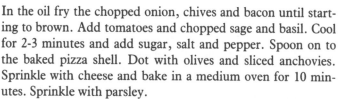

In the oil fry the chopped onion, chives and bacon until starting to brown. Add tomatoes and chopped sage and basil. Cool for 2-3 minutes and add sugar, salt and pepper. Spoon on to the baked pizza shell. Dot with olives and sliced anchovies. Sprinkle with cheese and bake in a medium oven for 10 minutes. Sprinkle with parsley.

Or Place all raw ingredients, well mixed, onto the uncooked yeast pizza, and bake on a baking sheet for 20 minutes to half an hour on the middle shelf of the oven at 180°C (350°F). Sprinkle with grated cheese and parsley just as the cooking time is up, and add olives and anchovies.

PANCAKES WITH HERBS

A variety of fillings can make pancakes the most versatile of all dishes. The batter below is a standard one and can be used for sweet or savory pancakes.

2 eggs, separated and whisked
250 ml (1 cup) wholewheat flour
250 ml (1 cup) cake flour
pinch or two of salt
250 ml (1 cup) water
15 ml (3 tsp) chopped herbs

Mix flour and water to a fairly thin batter. Add in the whisked egg yolks and the salt, then fold in the stiffly beaten egg whites. Add the herbs. Have ready two pans with a little hot oil in each. Pour a small quantity of batter into each pan. Turn the pan so it spreads evenly. Once it starts to bubble turn the pancake over or toss. Cook for half a minute or until it is golden. Keep a pot of boiling water on the stove with a plate over it. Place each pancake on the plate and cover with the lid of a casserole or pot. Prepare the filling.

Savory Pancakes

Into the standard batter stir any of the herbs listed below, chopping them finely:

tarragon, thyme, sage, parsley, chives, basil, comfrey, savory, marjoram, borage, chervil, celery, oreganum, watercress, lovage, fennel, dill, garlic, salad burnet.

Sweet Pancakes

For fruit or sweet fillings, or even just sprinkled with sugar and cinnamon and lemon juice, stir in any of the herbs listed below, chopping them finely:

scented geranium, lemon thyme, mint, rosemary, lemon balm.

Savory Filling (For 6 pancakes)

2 medium onions, finely chopped
5 ml (1 tsp) thyme
12,5 ml (1 tbsp) sugar
2-4 tomatoes, skinned and chopped
25 ml (2 tbsp) celery, chopped
250 g (8 oz) mushrooms, sliced
little oil
salt and pepper

Fry onions in the oil. Add celery and brown slightly. Add tomatoes, mushrooms, thyme, salt, pepper and sugar. Cook, covered, until soft. Add chopped parsley last of all. Spoon onto pancakes, roll up or fold over and serve with grated cheese handed separately.

Sweet Filling – Geranium Custard (For 6 pancakes)

750 ml (3 cups) milk
250 ml (1 cup) scented geranium leaves
125 ml (½ cup) brown sugar
2 eggs, beaten
25-37,5 ml (2-3 tbsp) custard powder

Boil up the milk and geranium leaves for 3-4 minutes, stirring all the time. Discard the geranium leaves. Add sugar and custard powder which has been mixed with a little cold milk. Stir all the time as it thickens, cooking over low heat. Slowly stirring or whisking, fold in the beaten eggs. Cook gently until thick. Pour over stewed apples or rhubarb, or use plain over the pancake. Roll up or fold over. Serve with whipped cream.

MACARONI CHEESE AND HERBS (Serves 4-6)

225 g (8 oz) wholewheat macaroni
200 g (7 oz/1 cup) cheddar cheese, coarsely grated
1 medium onion, finely chopped
1-2 large tomatoes, skinned and chopped
25 ml (2 tbsp) oreganum
25 ml (2 tbsp) chives
25 ml (2 tbsp) butter
175 g (6 oz) chopped, lean bacon
2 eggs, beaten
300 ml (1/2 pt/1 1/4 cups) milk
2 ml (1/2 tsp) paprika
5 ml (1 tsp) salt
190 ml (3/4 cup) breadcrumbs

Drop the macaroni into boiling salted water and boil briskly
for 7-10 minutes or until it is just tender. Drain. Grease a
casserole dish, place alternate layers macaroni, then tomato,
chives, oreganum, bacon and sprinkling of cheese, topping
with macaroni. Dot with butter. Whisk eggs into milk, add salt
and paprika, and pour over the macaroni mixture. Sprinkle
with breadcrumbs and the remaining cheese. Bake in a moder-
ate oven (180°C/350°F) for 40-45 minutes. Serve with fresh
watercress.

SAGE FRITTERS (Serves 8)

Use sage, borage, basil or comfrey leaves.

4-6 doz fresh sage leaves (double the batter for comfrey leaves)
37,5 ml (3 tbsp) butter
250-375 ml (1-1½ cups) cake flour
125-190 ml (½-¾ cup) milk
2 stiffly beaten egg whites
2 egg yolks, beaten
5 ml (1 tsp) salt and a little pepper

Wash and dry sage leaves. Melt butter in a saucepan, add 125 ml (½ cup) cold water and bring to the boil. Add milk. Set aside to cool. Combine flour and salt in a bowl. Gradually blend in the butter, water and milk mixture. Blend in the egg yolks and lastly fold in the egg whites. Dip the leaves into the batter, drop into a pan of hot oil 2,5 cm (1") deep. (Do not put too many into the pan at once.) Fry until golden brown. With a slotted spoon remove the fritters from the pan and drain on paper towels. Keep hot in the oven until all are cooked. Serve hot as a snack or as a side dish.

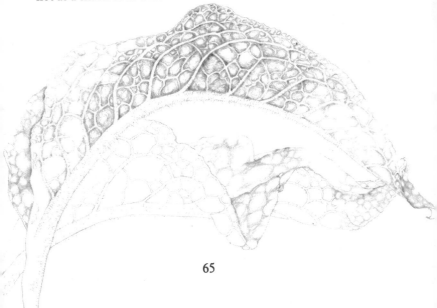

POTATO CAKES WITH MINT (Serves 4-6)

500 ml (2 cups) mashed potatoes
250 ml (1 cup) flour
salt and pepper to taste
125 ml (½ cup) chopped chives
25 ml (2 tbsp) chopped mint
25 ml (2 tbsp) butter
1 cup chopped borage leaves
1 egg, beaten
oil

Mix flour into the hot potato, a little at a time. Add the butter, chopped mint, chives and borage leaves. Mix well. Add salt and pepper and egg. Beat until fairly smooth. Take spoonfuls of the fairly stiff potato mixture and gently fry in a pan of hot oil. Turn over and brown. Serve with fried eggs and bacon or bean stew.

RICE AND ROSEMARY CASSEROLE (Serves 4-6)

2½ cups cooked brown rice
25 ml (2 tbsp) oil
12,5 ml (1 tbsp) chopped fresh rosemary
1 medium onion, finely chopped
25-37,5 ml (2-3 tbsp) chopped celery stalks and leaves
125 ml (½ cup) chopped parsley
375 ml (1½ cups) grated cheddar cheese
2 eggs, beaten in 500 ml (2 cups) milk
5 ml (1 tsp) salt and a little cayenne pepper
1 garlic clove, finely minced
butter

Fry the onion, celery and garlic in the oil until starting to brown. Add all the other ingredients but save a little grated cheese and the butter. Place in a buttered casserole, dot with butter and sprinkle the rest of the grated cheese over it. Bake at 180°C (350°F) for 20-30 minutes or until brown on top and bubbly round the sides. Serve with beef stew or bean stew.

Sweets and
Puddings

In winter a meal is deliciously rounded off with a sweet dish and these hot puddings below are heart-warming too, as they are quick and easy to make and will satisfy even the most jaded palate. Substitute different herbs if you like and don't be afraid to experiment with these basic recipes.

PUMPKIN FRITTERS (Serves 6)

It might be as well to double the quantities in this recipe before you begin – they are such favourites!

3 cups cooked pumpkin
190 ml (¾ cup) cake flour
3 eggs, beaten
12,5 ml (1 tbsp) lemon thyme
pinch salt
20 ml (4 tsp) baking powder
15 ml (3 tsp) cinnamon
250 ml (1 cup) brown sugar

Mix all ingredients together, except cinnamon and sugar. Drop spoonfuls of this mixture into a pan of hot oil, 2,5 cm (1") deep. Brown on both sides. Drain on paper towels. Mix cinnamon into the brown sugar. Roll each fritter in the mixture and sprinkle over the fritters.

Or Make a syrup:

500 ml (2 cups) brown sugar
250 ml (1 cup) water
250 ml (1 cup) milk
12,5 ml (1 tbsp) butter
10ml (2 tsp) cornflour

Stir the cornflour into the sugar and mix into the water. Add milk and butter. Place on the stove and boil up, stirring all the time, for two minutes. Place fritters in a serving dish and pour the syrup over them. Serve hot with a bowl of whipped cream.

VINEGAR AND SCENTED GERANIUM PUDDING
(Serves 6-8)

This pudding is equally delicious with lemon balm or scented geranium or lemon thyme, and it never fails!

500 ml (2 cups) flour
   (I use half brown and half cake flour)
250 ml (1 cup) brown sugar
250 ml (1 cup) butter
5 ml (1 tsp) ginger
8 geranium leaves or 15 ml (3 tsp) lemon thyme
1 egg, beaten
125 ml (½ cup) milk mixed with 5 ml
   (1 tsp) bicarbonate of soda
pinch salt
2 dessert spoons apricot jam

Rub butter into flour and add all the other ingredients except geranium leaves.

69

Syrup

Mix 60 ml (¼ cup) vinegar in 500 ml (2 cups) water and 250 ml (1 cup) sugar. Pour the syrup into a deep casserole. Pour the batter on top of the syrup. Place the geranium leaves on top. Bake at 180°C (350°F) for half an hour or until pudding starts to brown. Remove geranium leaves. Serve with custard or whipped cream.

RICE PUDDING WITH LEMON BALM (Serves 4-6)

This is one of the quickest and easiest puddings to make and can bake alongside the roast. It is also very nutritious and warming.

250 ml (1 cup) uncooked brown rice, soaked in 750 ml (3 cups)
*   boiling water for one hour*
500 ml (2 cups) milk
2 eggs, beaten
125 ml (½ cup) brown sugar or 25 ml (2 tbsp) honey
125 ml (½ cup) chopped almonds
125 ml (½ cup) seedless raisins
25 ml (2 tbsp) chopped lemon balm

Drain the rice and combine all ingredients. Pour into a baking dish. Sprinkle with cinnamon. Place, covered, in a medium oven at 180°C (350°F) for approximately one hour or until rice has cooked and the pudding starts to brown. Do not let it dry out. To speed up the process use 500 ml (2 cups) cooked rice and mix in all the ingredients as above. Serve with cream.

APPLE CRISP WITH PEPPERMINT (Serves 4-6)

4-6 large apples, peeled and sliced
10 ml (2 tsp) cinnamon
25 ml (2 tbsp) chopped peppermint
25 ml (2 tbsp) wholewheat flour
25 ml (2 tbsp) lemon juice
190 ml (¾ cup) seedless raisins
apple juice or water
125 ml (½ cup) brown sugar

Grease a large ovenproof baking dish. Mix the sliced apples with the flour, cinnamon, peppermint, brown sugar, raisins and lemon juice. Place in the baking dish. Pour over enough apple juice or water to cover the bottom (about 2 cups).

Topping

125 ml (½ cup) wholewheat flour
500 ml (1 cup) whole large flake oats
10 ml (2 tsp) cinnamon
125 ml (½ cup) brown sugar
125 ml (½ cup) butter

Mix the topping in a bowl, then press it on top of the apples. Dot with butter. Bake at 190°C (375°F) for 25 minutes or until apples are soft and it starts to brown. Serve with lashings of whipped cream.

HERB AND FRUIT TART (Serves up to 8)

This hot pudding can be made with pie apples, pineapple chunks, sliced peaches, apricots or rhubarb. Flavour with lemon thyme, melissa (lemon balm) or scented geranium, finely chopped.

500 ml (2 cups) wholewheat flour
25 ml (3 tsp) baking powder
250 ml (1 cup) brown sugar
37,5 ml (3 tbsp) butter
2 eggs, beaten
12,5 ml (1 tbsp) lemon thyme
25 ml (2 tbsp) lemon balm
pinch salt
4 apples, peeled and sliced
½ cup raisins
125-190 ml (½-¾ cup) milk

Boil up milk and butter with the raisins. Add flour, beaten egg, sugar and the herbs. Add baking powder and mix well. Spread apples out in a buttered baking dish and pour the batter over them. Bake at 190°C (375°F) for ½ hour or until firm. Meanwhile prepare a sauce:

250 ml (1 cup) sugar
125 ml (½ cup) coconut
25 ml (2 tbsp) butter
1 small tin unsweetened condensed milk

Boil up for two minutes. Pour over hot tart as it comes out of the oven. Serve warm with custard or whipped cream.

Bread, Biscuits and Cakes

Try adding herbs to old favourite recipes. The basic ones given here lend themselves to different herbs and to find pleasing combinations is only a matter of personal taste.

EASY BREAD

This is easy even if you have never baked bread before. If you like you can add 250 ml (1 cup) wheatgerm, sunflower seeds, soy flour or skim milk powder. Herbs such as thyme, rosemary, garlic, oreganum, parsley, etc (25-37,5 ml or 2-3 tbsp) can also be added.

625 ml (2½ cups) warm water
12,5 ml (1 tbsp) brown sugar
12,5 ml (1 tbsp) active dried yeast
6 cups wholewheat flour
12,5 ml (1 tbsp) salt

Pour the water into a large bowl and add the sugar and yeast. Let it stand for a few minutes and the yeast will start to bubble and froth. Let it rise and fill the bowl. Now stir in half the wholewheat flour. Beat well with a wooden spoon until the dough becomes smooth and stretchy. Add the salt and the rest of the flour little by little, all the time kneading it in the bowl until it is no longer sticky. Then turn it out onto a floured board. Knead until it is springy and smooth. Return to the bowl, cover, keep warm and allow it to rise to double size (about half an hour). Grease two loaf pans, divide the dough into two and mould into the shape of the bread pan. Cover with a clean cloth, keep warm and let the dough rise again to the top of the pans. Bake in a medum oven (190°C/375°F) for about 40 minutes or until they sound hollow when you knock. The loaves should be a rich golden brown.

QUICK HERB SCONES (Serves 4-6)

This is a basic scone dough to which currants, almonds or sunflower seeds (½ cup each) can be added, or 2 tablespoons of any savoury or sweet herb. Served with butter, they need to be hot to be enjoyed at their best.

500 ml (2 cups) wholewheat flour
20 ml (4 tsp) baking powder
80 ml (⅓ cup) oil
1 egg, beaten
250 ml (1 cup) milk and water, mixed
pinch salt
25 ml (2 tbsp) finely chopped scented geranium
125-190 ml (½-¾ cup) currants

Mix baking powder and flour. Add a little sugar – 125 ml (½ cup) if you want a sweet scone. Whisk milk, water, egg and oil and mix into flour. Add herbs and currants. Grease 12 muffin pans. Drop spoonfuls of this dough into the pans. Bake at 190°C (375°F) for 10 minutes. Split open and push butter and a little jam into each one.

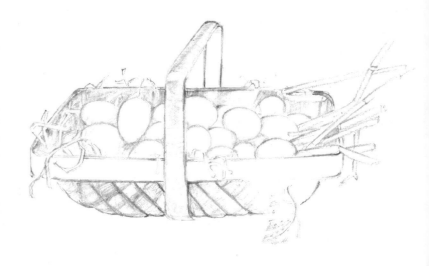

FOOLPROOF CHOCOLATE CAKE WITH MINT

This cake has been a family favourite for many years. It always turns out well and, with the addition of a most exciting mint known as 'chocolate mint' or spearmint, it is a party piece.

125 g (4 oz) dark chocolate, melted in 125 ml (½ cup) boiling
   water
250 ml (1 cup) butter
500 ml (2 cups) brown sugar
4 egg yolks
250 ml (1 cup) sour milk (mix 250 ml (1 cup) milk with 25 ml (2
   tbsp) vinegar)
7 egg whites, whisked
2 ml (½ tsp) salt
37,5 ml (3 tbsp) chopped chocolate mint
25 ml (2 tbsp) vanilla
50 ml (4 tbsp) baking powder
625 ml (2½ cups) mixed cake and wholewheat flour

Separate eggs and whisk whites stiffly. Cream butter and sugar. Add 4 egg yolks, one at a time, and beat well. Add melted chocolate and vanilla and milk alternately with flour into which the baking powder has been mixed. Mix well. Fold in egg whites and the chopped chocolate mint or spearmint. Line two 23 cm (9") cake tins with wax paper. Pour in the cake mixture. Bake for 40 minutes at 190°C (375°F) or until cake is done (test by inserting a skewer – when it comes out clean the cake is done). Turn out of pans and cool on a wire rack.

Filling and Topping

3 egg yolks
250 ml (1 cup) unsweetened evaporated milk
5 ml (1 tsp) vanilla
15 ml (3 tsp) finely chopped chocolate mint
250 ml (1 cup) brown sugar
25 ml (2 tbsp) butter
625 ml (2½ cups) coconut
125 ml (½ cup) chopped pecan nuts or almonds or walnuts

Mix all ingredients together, except coconut and nuts. Boil over low heat, stirring well until it begins to thicken. Add coconut and nuts. Use as a filling between the two cakes and as a topping, decorating with chocolate mint leaves and whole almonds.

ROSEMARY BISCUITS (Makes approximately 3 dozen)

150 ml (12 heaped tbsp) flour
75 ml (6 heaped tbsp) brown sugar
100 ml (8 tbsp) butter
2 eggs, beaten
15 ml (3 tsp) baking powder
pinch salt
37,5 ml (3 tbsp) chopped rosemary
crushed cornflakes or coconut

Blend sugar and butter. Beat in eggs, chopped rosemary and salt. Add flour and baking powder. Mix into a thick dough. Roll teaspoonfuls of the dough in crushed cornflakes or coconut, place on a greased baking sheet, equally spaced (allow 5 cm between each) and bake at 200°C (400°F) for 15 minutes.

WHOLEWHEAT HEALTH RUSKS

500 g (1 lb) butter – leave out of fridge overnight
9 cups wholewheat flour
1 packet allbran flakes or 4 cups bran
500 g honey
7 ml (1½ tsp) salt
1½ litres (6 cups) milk
3 dessertspoons baking powder
2 eggs
250 ml (1 cup) sunflower seeds

Mix flour, salt and baking powder. Rub in softened butter. Beat eggs into milk. Beat in honey. Add to dry ingredients. Add sunflower seeds and bran. Mix well. Spoon into 4 well-greased loaf tins. Bake at 180°C (350°F) for approximately one hour. Cool. Before going to bed slice the loaves into fairly thick fingers. Space them on wire cake coolers. Place in the oven, leave the door slightly open and bake at 60°-100°C (180°-200°F) overnight. Pack into tins when cool.

Winter
Drinks

Herbs can be drunk with enjoyment in the form of teas, particularly suited to cold winter days. A great variety of herbs can be used not only in making health drinks but also to combat winter colds and coughs and to aid fatigue.

Here is a list of my favourite herbs used in teas:
rosemary
sage
lemon balm (melissa)
fennel
mint
comfrey
scented geranium
lavender
winter savory
lemon thyme

HERB TEA

Take a thumb length sprig of your chosen herb (eg rosemary) and place in a cup. Pour boiling water over it. Steep for a few minutes. Remove herb, sweeten with honey if you like it sweet, and add a squeeze of lemon juice.

Some herbs (eg the mints and lemon thyme) need two or three sprigs. Large leaves like comfrey (wonderful for bronchitis, coughs and colds), fennel (also good for colds and an excellent slimming tea), scented geranium (to aid sleep and stress) can be chopped. Approximately 60 ml (¼ cup) of chopped herb is used to 250 ml (1 cup) boiling water. Your personal taste will soon ensure just the right amount. Combine and experiment.

83

MULLED ALE

This is an excellent pick-me-up tonic for the weary and for invalids and convalescents – or for a winter chill-remover!

625 ml (2½ cups) beer or stout
1 egg, beaten
12,5 ml (1 tbsp) brown sugar
2 ml (½ tsp) ground ginger
2 ml (½ tsp) grated nutmeg
2 ml (½ tsp) ground cinnamon
1 large sprig rosemary
1 large sprig sage

Boil up the spices, herbs and sugar in the beer. Remove from heat and stand covered until cool. Remove herbs and discard. Beat up the egg, add a little spiced beer, whisking well, then add this to the whole. Now reheat slowly, without boiling (if it boils it will curdle). Drink immediately. Serve this as a nightly drink to convalescents.

PORT NEGUS OR ROSEMARY WINE

Florence Nightingale was said to have given Port Negus to the sick and wounded in the Crimea. This is a health-giving drink. I make a bottle at a time and pour off and warm what is needed, allowing the rest to stand.

1 bottle red wine or port
1 stick cinnamon
1 whole nutmeg, crushed roughly
12,5-25 ml (1-2 tbsp) sugar
1 long sprig rosemary
3-6 sprigs lemon thyme

Heat the wine with all the ingredients to boiling point. Stand and cool. Pour into a bottle (herbs and spices still in it) and store. When a warming drink is needed, pour off sufficient and heat. Serve hot. (Winter savory can replace lemon thyme if desired.)

MULLED CIDER

570 ml-1 litre (1½-2 pt) apple juice
60-75 ml (5-6 tbsp) brown sugar
2 ml (½ tsp) salt
2 ml (½ tsp) ground cloves
2 ml (½ tsp) ground nutmeg
1 piece root ginger
2 ml (½ tsp) allspice
1 stick cinnamon
6 sprigs peppermint or ordinary mint

Mix all the ingredients in a heavy-bottomed pot and bring slowly to the boil. (Start on a very low heat.) Keep the pot covered throughout. Simmer gently for ten minutes. Remove from stove and stand. Strain through muslin when cool. Bottle and keep in fridge. Reheat when needed.

GINGER EGG WARMER (Serves 2)

This is a wonderful breakfast drink to start a bitter winter day.

500 ml (2 cups) milk
3 eggs
2 ml (1/2 tsp) ginger powder
25 ml (2 tbsp) honey
1 sprig sage
12,5 ml (1 tbsp) brandy (optional)

Boil up the milk with the ginger, honey and sage. Whisk the eggs. Remove the sage from the milk and slowly add the hot milk to the eggs, beating all the time. (If you add it too quickly it will curdle.) Lastly add the brandy and drink hot. This is also an excellent drink for elderly people and for convalescents.